brownies

brownies

Linda Collister photography by Richard Jung

RYLAND
PETERS
& SMALL

LONDON NEW YORK

First published in the
United Kingdom in 2006
by Ryland Peters & Small
20–21 Jockey's Fields
London WC1R 4BW
www.rylandpeters.com

10 9 8 7 6 5 4 3 2 1

ISBN-10: 1 84597 209 0
ISBN-13: 978 1 84597 209 7

A CIP record for this book is available
from the British Library.

Senior Designer Steve Painter
Commissioning Editor Julia Charles
Production Controller Eleanor Cant
Art Director Anne-Marie Bulat
Publishing Director Alison Starling
Food Stylist Linda Tubby
Props Stylist Roísín Nield
Index Hilary Bird

Notes
• All spoon measurements are level
unless otherwise specified.
• Ovens should be preheated to the
specified temperatures. All ovens work
slightly differently. I recommend using
an oven thermometer and suggest you
consult the maker's handbook for any
special instructions – particularly if you
are using a fan-assisted oven as you may
need to adjust cooking temperatures
according to manufacturer's instructions.

Author's acknowledgements
I would like to thank the many people
who helped with this book; Barbara Levy,
Steve Painter, Julia Charles, Richard Jung,
Linda Tubby and Roísín Nield.

contents

introduction

Chocolate brownies are both homely and decadent. They are quick and easy to put together, yet immensely rich and satisfying. So what makes a brownie different from cake? The texture is crucial; a good brownie should be soft, with a close, moist, fudgy quality completely unlike the crumbly, open and light texture of a sponge cake. For this reason it is always far better to undercook brownies slightly, than to overcook them.

It's well worth using the best quality chocolate you can find – choose bars made with around 70 per cent cocoa solids which will give a good depth of flavour. Cocoa powder is also often added to increase the intensity of flavour without adding more sugar. The same applies to white chocolate – use very good quality, not children's bars, for a deep flavour rather than a cloying sweetness.

I've included old-fashioned brownies plus some new ones that may shock the purists! Although the 'classic' brownies use pecans or walnuts, many of these recipes are nut-free. Some are 'grown-up' brownies with a dash of Kirsch or rum, some are muffins for lunchboxes and, because I like to serve brownies at the end of a meal, I've included some delicious desserts, as well as sauces. But, all you really need is a glass of cold milk or a hot cup of coffee and a square of brownie, warm from the oven.

making a classic brownie

If you've never made brownies before, this easy recipe
for a Classic Fudge Brownie will get you hooked. It's
the first one I ever made and it's a winner! Eat it warm
from the oven with a scoop of vanilla ice cream and
Chocolate Fudge Sauce (see page 61).

100 g good-quality plain chocolate,

125 g unsalted butter, softened

275 g caster sugar

1 teaspoon real vanilla essence

2 large free-range eggs, lightly beaten

85 g plain flour

2 tablespoons cocoa powder

100 g pecan halves or pieces

50 g good-quality plain chocolate, roughly chopped or plain choc chips

a brownie tin, 20.5 x 25.5 cm, greased and base-lined

Makes 20

Preheat the oven to 180°C (350°F) Gas 4. Break the 100 g chocolate into pieces and put it in a heatproof bowl. Set the bowl over a pan of steaming water and melt the chocolate gently, stirring frequently. Remove the bowl from the pan and leave to cool until needed.

Put the butter in a large mixing bowl and, using either a wooden spoon or an electric mixer, beat until soft and creamy. Add the sugar and vanilla and continue beating until the mixture is soft and fluffy. Gradually beat in the eggs then beat in the melted chocolate.

Sift the flour and cocoa onto the mixture and stir in. When thoroughly combined add the nuts and the chocolate pieces or choc chips and stir in. Transfer the mixture to the prepared tin and spread evenly.

Bake in the preheated oven for about 25 to 30 minutes until a skewer inserted halfway between the sides and the centre comes out just clean. Remove the tin from the oven. Leave to cool until just warm before removing from the tin and cutting into 20 pieces. Best eaten warm. Once cold, store in an airtight container and eat within 5 days.

brownies

Some brownie enthusiasts believe that only cocoa should be used, not melted plain chocolate, as it gives a deeper, truly intense chocolate flavour which balances the sugar necessary to give a proper fudgy texture. Choose the best quality cocoa you can find.

old-fashioned brownies

100 g walnut pieces

4 large free-range eggs

300 g caster sugar

140 g unsalted butter, melted

½ teaspoon real vanilla essence

140 g plain flour

75 g cocoa powder

a brownie tin, 20.5 x 25.5 cm, greased and base-lined

Makes 16

Preheat the oven to 170°C (325°F) Gas 3. Put the walnut pieces in an ovenproof dish and lightly toast in the oven for about 10 minutes. Remove from the oven and leave to cool. Don't turn off the oven.

Meanwhile break the eggs into a mixing bowl. Use a hand-held electric mixer to whisk until frothy then whisk in the sugar. Whisk for a minute then, still whisking constantly, add the melted butter in a steady stream. Whisk for a minute then whisk in the vanilla.

Sieve the flour and cocoa into the bowl and stir in with a wooden spoon. When thoroughly combined stir in the nuts. Transfer the mixture to the prepared tin and spread evenly.

Bake in the preheated oven for about 25 minutes until a skewer inserted halfway between the sides and the centre comes out just clean. Remove the tin from the oven.

Leave to cool completely before removing from the tin and cutting into 16 pieces. Store in an airtight container and eat within 5 days.

There's a lot of chocolate in this recipe, but it's not too sweet due to the cocoa content and the addition of either walnut or pecan pieces. These brownies are particularly good eaten warm with whipped cream.

very rich brownies

200 g good-quality plain chocolate

100 g unsalted butter, softened

250 g light brown muscovado sugar

4 large free-range eggs, lightly beaten

½ teaspoon real vanilla essence

60 g plain flour

60 g cocoa powder

100 g walnut or pecan pieces

chocolate shavings, to decorate

a brownie tin, 20.5 x 25.5 cm, greased and base-lined

Makes 20

Preheat the oven to 180°C (350°F) Gas 4. Break up the chocolate and put it in a heatproof bowl. Set the bowl over a pan of steaming water and gently melt the chocolate, stirring frequently. Remove the bowl from the pan and leave to cool until needed.

Put the soft butter and sugar into a mixing bowl and, using either a wooden spoon or an electric mixer, beat until fluffy. Gradually beat in the eggs then the vanilla. Next, beat in the melted chocolate. When thoroughly combined sift the flour and cocoa onto the mixture and stir in. Mix in the nuts then transfer to the prepared tin and spread evenly.

Bake in the preheated oven for about 20 minutes or until almost firm to the touch. Remove the tin from the oven.

Leave to cool before removing from the tin and cutting into 20 pieces. Serve sprinkled with chocolate shavings. (These can be made by grating dark chocolate using the coarse hole side of a grater.) Store in an airtight container and eat within 4 days.

Black cherries, Kirsch and dark, rich chocolate are a classic combination. Here, stoned black cherries preserved in a Kirsch syrup are dropped into a well-flavoured, not too sweet, double-chocolate brownie mixture. It makes a perfect dessert for a New Year's party, when fruits preserved in alcohol are readily available from supermarkets. For an alcohol-free alternative use black cherries canned in either juice or light syrup. Delicious served with Crème Chantilly (see page 44).

black forest brownies

225 g good-quality plain chocolate

125 g unsalted butter, diced

3 tablespoons double cream

3 large free-range eggs

225 g caster sugar

2 tablespoons Kirsch or Kirsch syrup from a jar of preserved cherries (optional)

160 g plain flour

100 g good-quality plain chocolate, roughly chopped or plain choc chips

465-g jar or can black cherries (175 g drained weight)

icing sugar, for dusting

a brownie tin, 20.5 x 25.5 cm, greased and base-lined

Makes 24

Preheat the oven to 180°C (350°F) Gas 4. Break up the 225 g chocolate and put it in a heatproof bowl. Add the diced butter and cream to the bowl and set it over a pan of steaming water. Melt gently, stirring frequently. Remove the bowl from the pan and leave to cool until needed.

Break the eggs into the bowl of an electric mixer and whisk just until frothy. Add the sugar and Kirsch (if using) and whisk until thick and mousse-like. Whisk in the melted chocolate mixture.

Sift the flour onto the mixture and stir in. When thoroughly combined stir in the pieces of chocolate. Transfer the mixture to the prepared tin and spread evenly. Gently drop the cherries onto the brownie mixture, spacing them as evenly as possible.

Bake in the preheated oven for 30 to 35 minutes until a skewer inserted halfway between the sides and the centre comes out just clean. Remove the tin from the oven.

Leave until cool before removing from the tin and cutting into 24 pieces. Serve dusted with icing sugar. Store in an airtight container and eat within 4 days.

Walnuts have a creamy, bittersweet taste that contrasts well with the sweetness of the brownie mixture. Here, there is a high proportion of walnuts to mixture, plus a fudgy walnut topping. For a deeper flavour toast the nuts for 10 minutes in the oven before adding to both the brownie and topping mixtures.

extra-nutty brownies

100 g good-quality plain chocolate

115 g unsalted butter

200 g light brown muscovado sugar

½ teaspoon real vanilla essence

2 large free-range eggs, lightly beaten

100 g plain flour

2 tablespoons cocoa powder

150 g walnut pieces

Icing:

50 g good-quality plain chocolate

50 g unsalted butter

2 tablespoons milk

2 tablespoons cocoa powder

100 g icing sugar

50 g walnut pieces

a brownie tin, 20.5 x 25.5 cm, greased and base-lined

Makes 20

Preheat the oven to 180°C (350°F) Gas 4. Break up the chocolate and put it in a heatproof mixing bowl with the butter. Set the bowl over a pan of steaming water and melt gently, stirring frequently.

Remove the bowl from the pan and stir in the sugar and vanilla. Add the eggs and beat well with a wooden spoon until the mixture comes together as a smooth batter.

Sift the flour and cocoa into the bowl and stir in. When thoroughly combined stir in the nuts. Transfer the mixture to the prepared tin and spread evenly.

Bake in the preheated oven for about 15 minutes or until just firm to the touch. Remove the tin from the oven. Leave to cool completely then carefully remove the brownie from the tin.

Meanwhile make the icing: melt the chocolate and butter as above. Remove the bowl from the pan and stir in the milk.

Sift the cocoa and icing sugar into the bowl and stir in. When thick and smooth stir in the nuts. Spread the icing over the cooled, baked brownie.

Once the topping is firm, cut the brownie into 20 pieces. Store in an airtight container and eat within 4 days.

The sharpness of dried cranberries balances the sweetness of this dark chocolate brownie mixture, and the tangy grated orange zest lifts the richness.

cranberry and dark chocolate brownies

200 g good-quality plain chocolate

200 g unsalted butter, diced

3 large free-range eggs

175 g caster sugar

grated zest of 1 medium unwaxed orange

200 g plain flour

100 g dried cranberries

a brownie tin, 20.5 x 25.5 cm, greased and base-lined

Makes 20

Preheat the oven to 180°C (350°F) Gas 4. Break up the chocolate and put it in a heatproof mixing bowl with the butter. Set the bowl over a pan of steaming water and melt gently, stirring frequently. Remove the bowl from the pan and leave to cool until needed.

Whisk the eggs until frothy using an electric mixer or whisk. Add the sugar and orange zest and whisk until the mixture becomes very thick and mousse-like. Whisk in the melted chocolate mixture.

Sift the flour onto the mixture and stir in. When everything is thoroughly combined stir in the dried cranberries. Transfer the mixture to the prepared tin and spread evenly.

Bake in the preheated oven for about 25 minutes or until a skewer inserted halfway between the sides and the centre comes out just clean. Remove the tin from the oven.

Leave to cool before removing from the tin and cutting into 20 pieces. Store in an airtight container and eat within 5 days.

Ginger and chocolate is a delicious taste combination. Here very good dark chocolate flavoured with pieces of crystallized ginger is used in a dark chocolate mixture. Just a hint of spice, plus deliciously tangy sour cream, makes these brownies extra special.

sour cream and spice brownies

200 g good-quality plain chocolate

100 g unsalted butter

4 large free-range eggs

200 g caster sugar

100 g plain flour

¼ teaspoon ground cinnamon

½ teaspoon ground ginger

3 tablespoons sour cream

50 g bar plain chocolate with ginger pieces, chopped

a brownie tin, 20.5 x 25.5 cm, greased and base-lined

Makes 20

Preheat the oven to 180°C (350°F) Gas 4. Break up the plain chocolate and put it in a heatproof mixing bowl with the butter. Set the bowl over a pan of steaming water and melt gently, stirring frequently. Remove the bowl from the pan and leave to cool until needed.

Put the eggs and sugar into the bowl of an electric mixer and whisk until very thick and mousse-like. Whisk in the melted chocolate mixture.

Sift the flour and spices into the bowl and stir in. Mix in the sour cream followed by the chopped chocolate with ginger. Transfer to the prepared tin and spread evenly.

Bake in the preheated oven for about 25 minutes or until a skewer inserted halfway between the sides and the centre comes out just clean. Remove the tin from the oven.

Leave to cool before removing from the tin and cutting into 20 pieces. Store in an airtight container and eat within 5 days.

This brownie is rich and fudgy with masses of chocolate, plus a good shot of strong espresso coffee to offset the sweetness. Serve with a little pouring cream and you have an elegant dessert.

espresso brownies

230 g good-quality plain chocolate

115 g unsalted butter, softened

300 g caster sugar

5 large free-range eggs, lightly beaten

4 tablespoons strong espresso coffee, room temperature

70 g plain flour

70 g cocoa powder, plus extra for dusting

a brownie tin, 20.5 x 25.5 cm, greased and base-lined

Makes 20

Preheat the oven to 180°C (350°F) Gas 4. Break up the chocolate and put it in a heatproof bowl. Set the bowl over a pan of steaming water and melt gently, stirring frequently. Remove the bowl from the pan and leave to cool until needed.

Put the soft butter and sugar into the bowl of an electric mixer and beat until light and fluffy. Alternatively, you can also use a mixing bowl and wooden spoon. Gradually beat in the eggs, then the coffee.

Sift the flour and cocoa into the bowl and stir in. Add the cooled melted chocolate and mix in. When thoroughly combined transfer the mixture to the prepared tin and spread evenly.

Bake in the preheated oven for about 25 minutes or until a skewer inserted halfway between the sides and the centre comes out just clean. Remove the tin from the oven.

Leave to cool for 10 minutes before lightly dusting with cocoa powder, removing from the tin and cutting into 20 pieces. Serve warm or at room temperature with a jug of cream. Once cool, store in an airtight container and eat within 5 days.

A simple all-in-one recipe that owes its lovely, intense flavour to plain chocolate flavoured with good, strong coffee. This chocolate is most often sold in bars labelled as 'espresso chocolate'.

easy mocha brownies

100 g dark 'espresso' chocolate

175 g unsalted butter, diced

225 g caster sugar

3 large free-range eggs, lightly beaten

50 g plain flour

150 g walnut pieces

a brownie tin, 20.5 x 20.5 cm, greased and base-lined

Makes 9

Preheat the oven to 180°C (350°F) Gas 4. Break up the chocolate and put it in a heatproof mixing bowl with the butter. Set the bowl over a pan of steaming water and leave to melt gently, stirring very frequently.

Remove the bowl from the pan and stir in the sugar. Stir in the beaten eggs. When thoroughly combined stir in the flour, then finally mix in the nuts. Transfer the mixture to the prepared tin and spread evenly.

Bake in the preheated oven for about 25 to 30 minutes or until a skewer inserted halfway between the sides and the centre comes out just clean. Remove the tin from the oven.

Leave to cool before removing from the tin and cutting into 9 large pieces. Store in an airtight container and eat within 5 days.

These to-die-for brownies are incredibly rich in chocolate and not too sweet. This is a very useful recipe when you need a flour-free dessert or cake. Undercooking is vital to avoid a crumbly texture.

flourless-yet-fudgy brownies

300 g good-quality plain chocolate

150 g unsalted butter, diced

50 g cocoa powder, sifted

4 large free-range eggs

200 g caster sugar

100 g walnut or pecan pieces

icing sugar, for dusting

a brownie tin, 20.5 x 25.5 cm, greased and base-lined

Makes 12

Preheat the oven to 180°C (350°F) Gas 4. Break up the chocolate and put it in a heatproof bowl with the butter. Set the bowl over a pan of steaming hot water and melt gently, stirring frequently. Remove the bowl from the pan and stir in the cocoa. Set aside until needed.

Put the eggs into a mixing bowl and beat well with a whisk or an electric mixer. Add the sugar and whisk thoroughly until very light and frothy and doubled in volume.

Using a large metal spoon, carefully fold in the chocolate mixture followed by the nuts. Transfer the mixture to the prepared tin and spread evenly.

Bake in the preheated oven for about 25 to 30 minutes until the top of the brownie is just firm to the touch but the centre is still slightly soft.

Leave to cool for 10 minutes before carefully removing from the tin. Dust with icing sugar before cutting into 12 pieces. Serve warm or at room temperature with a generous spoonful of sour cream or crème fraîche. Once cool, store in an airtight container and eat within 4 days.

peanut butter brownies

Chocolate and peanuts is a classic combination. This recipe is included by popular demand from my American family. I always use a top-quality peanut butter with no added sugar or fat as it gives the best flavour.

100 g good-quality plain chocolate

175 g unsalted butter, diced

3 large free-range eggs

200 g light brown muscovado sugar

120 g plain flour

2 tablespoons cocoa powder

Peanut mixture:

180 g smooth peanut butter

50 g caster sugar

1 tablespoon plain flour

5 tablespoons milk

2 tablespoons roasted, unsalted peanuts

a brownie tin, 20.5 x 25.5 cm, greased and base-lined

Makes 16

Preheat the oven to 180°C (350°F) Gas 4. Break up the chocolate and put it in a heatproof bowl with the butter. Set the bowl over a pan of steaming hot water and melt gently, stirring frequently. Remove the bowl from the pan and leave to cool until needed.

Break the eggs into a mixing bowl and beat well with a whisk or an electric mixer. Add the sugar and whisk until the mixture is very thick and mousse-like.

Whisk in the melted chocolate mixture. Sift the flour and cocoa onto the mixture and mix until thoroughly combined. Transfer the mixture to the prepared tin and spread evenly.

Put all the ingredients for the peanut mixture into a bowl and mix well. Drop teaspoonfuls of this mixture, evenly spaced, onto the chocolate mixture. Use the end of a chopstick or teaspoon handle to marble or swirl both mixtures. Scatter the peanuts over the top.

Bake in the preheated oven for about 30 minutes or until just firm. Leave to cool before removing from the tin and cutting into 16 pieces. Store in an airtight container and eat within 5 days.

This recipe is for my husband, who came across these unusual brownies in a San Francisco deli and begged me to make them for him at home. You'll need a box (or bar) of bittersweet dark chocolate with a soft, mint-flavoured fondant centre, of the type that is most often sold as 'after-dinner' mints.

mint brownies

125 g good-quality plain chocolate

100 g unsalted butter, diced

3 large free-range eggs

200 g caster sugar

100 g plain flour

2 tablespoons cocoa powder

100 g–200 g bittersweet dark chocolate with mint centre (depending on strength of flavour required)

a brownie tin, 20.5 x 25.5 cm, greased

Makes 20

Preheat the oven to 180°C (350°F) Gas 4. Break up the plain chocolate and put it in a heatproof bowl with the butter. Set the bowl over a pan of steaming water and melt gently, stirring frequently. Remove the bowl from the pan and set aside to cool until needed.

Whisk the eggs using an electric mixer or whisk then add the sugar and whisk until thick and mousse-like.

Whisk in the melted chocolate mixture. Sift the flour and cocoa onto the mixture and stir in. When thoroughly combined spoon half the brownie mixture into the prepared tin and spread evenly.

Leave the mint chocolates whole or break them up (depending on the size of the ones you are using). Arrange them over the brownie mixture already in the tin. Spoon the remaining brownie mixture on top and gently spread to cover the chocolate mints.

Bake in the preheated oven for about 25 minutes or until a skewer inserted halfway between the sides and the centre comes out just clean (though some of the sticky mint layer will appear). Remove the tin from the oven.

Leave to cool before removing from the tin and cutting into 20 pieces. Store in an airtight container and eat within 5 days.

These dark, double-chocolate brownies have a light texture and are subtly flavoured with rum. Serve them with vanilla ice cream for a perfect dessert.

choc choc rum brownies

60 g good quality plain chocolate

85 g unsalted butter, softened

200 g icing sugar

2 large free-range eggs, lightly beaten

2 tablespoons dark rum

60 g plain flour

100 g good-quality plain chocolate, finely chopped or plain choc chips

50 g walnut pieces

a brownie tin, 20.5 x 25.5 cm, greased and base-lined

Makes 16

Preheat the oven to 180°C (350°F) Gas 4. Break up the 60 g plain chocolate and put it in a heatproof bowl. Set the bowl over a pan of steaming water and melt gently, stirring frequently. Remove the bowl from the pan and leave to cool until needed.

Put the soft butter and icing sugar into the bowl of an electric mixer and beat until light and creamy, using slow speed at first. Alternatively, use a mixing bowl and wooden spoon.

Gradually beat in the eggs, followed by the rum. Scrape down the sides then beat in the melted chocolate. Stir in the flour, and when thoroughly combined, add the chopped chocolate or the choc chips and the nuts and mix thoroughly. Transfer the mixture to the prepared tin and spread evenly.

Bake in the preheated oven for about 20 to 25 minutes until the top is set and firm. Leave to cool before removing from the tin – taking care as the crust is fragile – and cutting into 16 pieces.

Serve warm or at room temperature. Once cool, store in an airtight container and eat within 4 days.

brownie 'muffins'

My children asked for a brownie that could survive life in a
school lunchbox. It needed to be nut-free, not too big and,
most importantly, not fall apart. I came up with this delicious
brownie-style muffin packed with choc chips and baked in
a paper case. The perfect solution!

2 large free-range eggs

125 g light brown muscovado sugar

125 g unsalted butter, melted

230 ml milk

½ teaspoon real vanilla essence

225 g plain flour

50 g cocoa powder

½ teaspoon baking powder

25 g white choc chips, plus extra to decorate

25 g plain or milk choc chips, plus extra to decorate

a 12-cup muffin tray, lined with 12 paper cases

Makes 12

Preheat the oven to 180°C (350°F) Gas 4. Break the eggs into a mixing bowl, add the sugar and beat with a wooden spoon until thoroughly combined. Beat in the melted butter, followed by the milk and the vanilla.

Sift the flour, cocoa and baking powder onto the mixture and mix in. Finally, stir in the choc chips. Divide the mixture equally between the paper cases and sprinkle a few extra choc chips on the top of each muffin to decorate.

Bake in the preheated oven for about 20 to 25 minutes until just firm to the touch. The brownies will only rise slightly and won't resemble peaked muffins.

Remove from the oven and allow to cool on a wire cooling tray. Store in an airtight container and eat within 5 days.

blondies

This Australian recipe is packed with rich, buttery macadamia nuts. For the best flavour use nuts from an unopened pack as they spoil quickly.

macadamia and white chocolate blondies

175 g good-quality white chocolate, chopped

115 g unsalted butter, diced

100 g caster sugar

2 large free-range eggs, lightly beaten

½ teaspoon real vanilla essence

130 g plain flour

½ teaspoon baking powder

150 g macadamia nuts, roughly chopped

100 g good-quality dark or white chocolate, roughly chopped or plain or white choc chips

a brownie tin, 20.5 x 25.5 cm, greased and base-lined

Makes 20

Preheat the oven to 180°C (350°F) Gas 4. Put the 175 g of chopped white chocolate and the diced butter into a heatproof mixing bowl, then set over a pan of steaming water. Melt gently, stirring frequently.

Remove the bowl from the pan and stir in the sugar with a wooden spoon – don't worry if the mixture looks curdled. Gradually stir in the beaten eggs, then the vanilla and beat for a minute until the mixture becomes thick, smooth and glossy.

Sift the flour and baking powder onto the mixture and stir in. When thoroughly combined stir in 100 g of the chopped nuts, and the 100 g chocolate or choc chips.

Transfer the mixture to the prepared tin and spread evenly. Scatter the remaining 50 g of nuts over the top.

Bake in the preheated oven for about 20 to 25 minutes or until light golden brown and a skewer inserted halfway between the sides and the centre comes out just clean.

Leave to cool before removing from the tin and cutting into 20 pieces. Store in an airtight container and eat within 4 days.

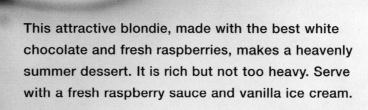

This attractive blondie, made with the best white chocolate and fresh raspberries, makes a heavenly summer dessert. It is rich but not too heavy. Serve with a fresh raspberry sauce and vanilla ice cream.

white chocolate and raspberry blondies

250 g good-quality white chocolate

200 g unsalted butter, diced

3 large free-range eggs

150 g caster sugar

½ teaspoon real vanilla essence

200 g plain flour

1 teaspoon baking powder

150 g fresh raspberries

a brownie tin, 20.5 x 20.5 cm, greased and base-lined

Makes 9

Preheat the oven to 180°C (350°F) Gas 4. Break up 150 g of the chocolate and put it in a heatproof mixing bowl with the butter. Set the bowl over a pan of steaming water. Melt gently, stirring frequently. Remove the bowl from the pan and leave to cool until needed.

Break the eggs into the bowl of an electric mixer or a mixing bowl. Whisk until frothy then add the sugar and the vanilla and beat thoroughly until very thick and mousse-like.

Whisk in the melted chocolate mixture. Sift the flour and baking powder onto the mixture and fold in. Chop the rest of the chocolate into pieces the size of your little fingernail and stir them in. Spoon the mixture into the prepared tin and spread evenly. Scatter the fresh raspberries over the top.

Bake in the preheated oven for about 25 minutes or until a skewer inserted halfway between the sides and the centre comes out just clean. Leave to cool before removing from the tin and cutting into 9 large pieces. Store in an airtight container and eat within 2 days.

coconut blondies

Slightly sticky and very chewy, these delicious blondies are heavy with coconut as well as plain and white chocolate. You will need to use the unsweetened type of desiccated coconut.

175 g unsweetened desiccated coconut

175 g unsalted butter

300 g light muscovado sugar

2 large free-range eggs, lightly beaten

1 teaspoon real vanilla essence

200 g plain flour

1 teaspoon baking powder

50 g good-quality white chocolate, chopped or white choc chips

50 g good-quality plain chocolate, chopped or plain choc chips

a brownie tin, 20.5 x 25.5 cm, greased and base-lined

Makes 20

Preheat the oven to 180°C (350°F) Gas 4. Put the coconut into a heatproof baking dish and toast in the preheated oven for about 5 minutes, stirring frequently, until a light golden brown. Remove from the oven and leave to cool. Leave the oven on.

Melt the butter in a medium-sized pan over low heat. Remove the pan from the heat and stir in the sugar with a wooden spoon.

Gradually beat in the eggs then the vanilla. Sift the flour and baking powder onto the mixture and stir in. Finally, work in the coconut and both the white and plain chopped chocolate or choc chips.

When everything is thoroughly combined transfer the mixture to the prepared tin and spread evenly.

Bake in the preheated oven for about 20 to 25 minutes or until golden brown and a skewer inserted halfway between the sides and the centre comes out just clean.

Leave to cool before removing from the tin and cutting into 20 pieces. Store in an airtight container and eat within 5 days.

This blondie doesn't contain any nuts but if you want to add some, simply replace the plain chocolate with 100 g of walnut halves or chopped Brazil nuts.

butterscotch blondies

115 g unsalted butter

230 g light brown muscovado sugar

2 large free-range eggs, lightly beaten

½ teaspoon real vanilla essence

180 g plain flour

½ teaspoon baking powder

100 g good-quality plain chocolate, chopped or plain choc chips

a brownie tin, 20.5 x 25.5 cm, greased and base-lined

Makes 20

Preheat the oven to 180°C (350°F) Gas 4. Put the butter in a medium-sized saucepan and melt gently over low heat.

Remove the pan from the heat and stir in the sugar with a wooden spoon. Gradually stir in the eggs then the vanilla and beat for a minute.

Sift the flour and baking powder onto the mixture and stir in. Add the chocolate pieces or choc chips (or nuts if using) and stir until thoroughly combined. Transfer the mixture to the prepared tin and spread evenly.

Bake in the preheated oven for about 25 minutes until light golden brown and a skewer inserted halfway between the sides and the centre comes out just clean.

Leave to cool before removing from the tin and cutting into 20 pieces. Store in an airtight container and eat within 5 days.

Crème Chantilly: To make this light, slightly sweetened whipped cream, first chill a whisk and mixing bowl for an hour in the fridge or freezer. Put 200 ml of whipping or double cream, well chilled, into the bowl. Whisk until thickened. Add ½ teaspoon of real vanilla essence and 1½ tablespoons of caster sugar. Whisk again until the cream is very thick and forms soft peaks. Stop at this point to avoid overwhipping then pile the cream into a bowl and serve immediately or cover and chill for up to 2 hours.

This is a deliciously moist and chewy little blondie packed with pecan halves, rather than pieces.

cinnamon pecan blondies

100 g unsalted butter

300 g light brown muscovado sugar

½ teaspoon ground cinnamon

2 large free-range eggs, lightly beaten

150 g plain flour

1 teaspoon baking powder

100 g pecan halves

a brownie tin, 20.5 x 25.5 cm, greased and base-lined

Makes 30

Preheat the oven to 180°C (350°F) Gas 4. Put the butter in a medium-sized pan. Set it over low heat and melt gently. Add the sugar and cinnamon and stir until smooth and melted. Remove the pan from the heat and leave to cool for a couple of minutes.

Use a wooden spoon to stir in the eggs, beating the mixture well until thoroughly combined. Sift the flour and baking powder onto the mixture, then stir in.

Mix in the pecans then transfer the mixture to the prepared tin and spread evenly.

Bake in the preheated oven for about 25 minutes until golden brown and a skewer inserted halfway between the sides and the centre comes out just clean.

Leave to cool for 5 minutes then loosen and remove from the tin. Wait until it is completely cold before cutting into 30 pieces. Store in an airtight container and eat within 4 days.

Incredibly rich and very moreish! This recipe uses cream cheese instead of butter and then half the mixture is flavoured with white chocolate, the rest with plain chocolate. Walnuts are added at the end to give a contrast in taste and texture.

half blondie, half brownie

100 g good-quality plain chocolate

50 g good-quality white chocolate

300 g full-fat cream cheese

200 g caster sugar

3 large free-range eggs

1 teaspoon real vanilla essence

100 g plain flour

100 g walnut pieces

a brownie tin, 20.5 x 25.5 cm, greased and base-lined

Makes 30

Preheat the oven to 180°C (350°F) Gas 4. Break up the plain chocolate and put it in a heatproof bowl. Set the bowl over a pan of steaming water and melt gently, stirring frequently. Remove the bowl from the pan and leave to cool until needed. Melt the white chocolate in the same way and leave to cool.

Put the cream cheese into the bowl of an electric mixer or food processor. Add the sugar and beat or process until smooth. Beat in the eggs, one at a time, then the vanilla. Work in the flour on low speed or using the 'pulse' button.

Transfer half the mixture to another bowl. Add the melted plain chocolate to one portion and mix thoroughly. Mix the melted white chocolate into the other portion. The plain chocolate mixture will be stiffer than the white.

Using a tablespoon, drop spoonfuls of the plain chocolate mixture into the prepared tin, spacing them evenly apart, with gaps between the blobs. Pour or spoon the white chocolate mixture over the top to fill the spaces. Scatter the nuts over the top. Use the end of a chopstick or the handle of a teaspoon to marble and swirl the two mixtures together.

Bake in the preheated oven for 25 to 30 minutes or until a skewer inserted halfway between the sides and the centre comes out just clean.

Leave to cool before removing from the tin and cutting into 30 pieces. Store in an airtight container and eat within 5 days.

brownie desserts

This deliciously gooey brownie pudding is an ideal recipe for absolute beginners. If you have suitable oven to tableware it can be made, baked and served in the same dish so it's a treat for chocolate lovers and washer uppers alike!

brownie lava pudding

50 g pecan pieces

100 g good-quality plain chocolate

115 g unsalted butter, diced

175 g caster sugar

2 large free-range eggs, lightly beaten

½ teaspoon real vanilla essence

75 g plain flour

a flameproof, ovenproof baking dish, approximately 18 cm (across top) and 7 cm deep

Serves 4 to 6

Preheat the oven to 180°C (350°F) Gas 4. Put the pecan pieces into an ovenproof dish and lightly toast in the preheated oven for about 10 minutes. Leave to cool.

Meanwhile break up the chocolate and put it in the baking dish (or in a medium-sized saucepan). Add the butter and melt gently over very, very low heat, stirring frequently.

Remove from the heat and stir in the sugar, then gradually stir in the eggs followed by the vanilla.

When thoroughly mixed, stir in the flour, then finally the nuts. When there are no floury streaks scrape down the sides of the dish (if using) so mixture doesn't scorch and put the dish into the preheated oven. Alternatively, if using a pan, transfer the mixture to a buttered ovenproof dish.

Bake for about 30 minutes until the mixture is set on top with a soft gooey layer at the bottom.

Serve immediately with a jug of fresh cream for pouring, or vanilla ice cream on the side.

Baking a brownie mixture in a crisp pastry case means you can make a very soft, sticky, nutty brownie. This recipe is a family favourite and I always bake it as one of our Thanksgiving pies.

brownie fudge pie

Pastry:

175 g plain flour

a pinch of salt

115 g unsalted butter,
chilled and diced

2–3 tablespoons ice cold water

Filling:

3 large free-range eggs

150 g light brown muscovado
sugar

150 g dark brown muscovado
sugar

½ teaspoon real vanilla essence

175 g unsalted butter, melted

50 g plain flour

50 g cocoa powder

150 g pecan halves or pieces

*a 23-cm loose-based flan tin
greaseproof paper
baking beans*

Serves 10

Preheat the oven to 180°C (350°F) Gas 4. To make the pastry in a food processor put the flour, salt and diced butter in the bowl and process until the mixture resembles fine crumbs. With the machine running add just enough water through the feed tube to make a slightly firm dough. Alternatively, make the pastry by hand: put the flour, salt and butter into a mixing bowl. Rub the pieces of butter into the flour with your fingertips until the mixture looks like fine crumbs. With a round-bladed knife stir in just enough water to bring the mixture together to make a slightly firm dough.

Wrap and chill for 15 minutes then roll out on a lightly-floured worksurface to a circle about 28 cm across and use to line the flan tin. Prick the bottom of the pastry case all over with a fork then chill for 15 minutes. Line the pastry case with greaseproof paper, fill with baking beans or rice to weight the paper down and bake 'blind' in the preheated oven for 12 to 15 minutes until lightly golden and just firm. Carefully remove the paper and beans and bake for a further 5 minutes or until the base is crisp and lightly golden. Remove from the oven and leave to cool while making the filling.

Break the eggs into the bowl of an electric mixer. Whisk until frothy then add the sugar and whisk until very thick and mousse-like. Add the vanilla and whisk again to combine. Whisk in the melted butter. Remove the bowl from the mixer and sift the flour and cocoa onto the mixture. Fold in with a large metal spoon. When there are no streaks of flour left, gently stir in the pecans. Transfer the mixture into the pastry case and spread evenly. Bake in the preheated oven for about 30 minutes or until firm to the touch. Remove from the oven.

Allow to cool slightly before removing from the tin. Serve warm with ice cream or Crème Chantilly (see page 44). Store at room temperature in a covered container and eat within 5 days.

This special dessert is very easy to prepare using a food processor. The base is a thick, rich, brownie and the topping is a luxuriously deep chocolate cheesecake with pecans.

brownie cheesecake

Preheat the oven to 170°C (325°C) Gas 3. First make the base: put the pieces of butter, sugar, flour and cocoa into the bowl of a food processor and process until the mixture comes together to make a thick paste.

Tip this mixture into the prepared tin and press onto the base to make a thick, even layer. Chill while making the topping.

Break up the chocolate and put it in a heatproof bowl. Set the bowl over a pan of steaming water and melt gently, stirring frequently. Remove the bowl from the pan and stir until smooth. Leave for 5 minutes to cool.

Put the cream cheese, eggs, sugar and vanilla into the bowl of the food processor. Process until thoroughly combined, scraping down the sides from time to time.

With the machine running add the cream through the feed tube, followed by the melted chocolate. When completely mixed pour the mixture onto the base and spread evenly. Finish by scattering over the pecans.

Stand the tin on a baking tray then bake in the preheated oven for 40 minutes until just firm. Turn off the oven but leave the cheesecake in the oven, without opening the door, to cool down. Then remove the cheesecake from the oven and chill at least 4 hours (preferably overnight) before removing from the tin. Dust with cocoa and serve.

Store in an airtight container in the fridge and eat within 5 days.

Base:

250 g unsalted butter, chilled and diced

250 g caster sugar

200 g plain flour

50 g cocoa powder

Topping:

200 g good-quality plain chocolate

400 g full-fat cream cheese

2 large free-range eggs

60 g caster sugar

½ teaspoon real vanilla essence

200 ml double cream

50 g pecan halves

cocoa powder, for dusting

a 23-cm spring-clip tin, greased

Serves 12

My son recently asked for this as his birthday cake, along with a large jug of Creamy Chocolate Sauce. Here an easy all-in-one brownie mixture is made thinner and more pliable than usual, then sliced up and sandwiched with vanilla ice cream. Note that it must be frozen for at least six hours before serving.

brownie ice cream cake

200 g good-quality plain chocolate

75 g unsalted butter, diced

2 tablespoons water

150 g caster sugar

2 large free-range eggs, lightly beaten

½ teaspoon real vanilla essence

100 g plain flour

½ teaspoon baking powder

75 g toasted almonds, finely chopped

To assemble:

1 litre good-quality vanilla ice-cream

a Swiss roll tin, 30.5 x 20.5cm, greased and base-lined

Serves 8

Preheat the oven to 170°C (325°F) Gas 3. Break up the chocolate and put in a heatproof mixing bowl with the butter and water. Set the bowl over a pan of steaming water and melt gently, stirring frequently.

Add the sugar to the melted mixture and stir well to thoroughly combine. Remove the bowl from the pan and leave to cool for a couple of minutes.

Stir in the eggs and vanilla and mix well. Sift the flour and baking powder onto the mixture and mix in. Finally, stir in the nuts. Transfer the mixture to the prepared tin and spread evenly.

Bake in the preheated oven for about 15 to 20 minutes or until a skewer inserted in to the centre of the mixture comes out just clean. Leave to cool completely in the tin then turn out onto a cutting board.

Cut the brownie in half lengthways to make 2 long strips. Cut one of the strips into 8 equal pieces. Wrap the long strip and the 8 top pieces in foil and freeze until firm. When ready to assemble transfer the ice cream to the fridge to slightly soften (it must not be allowed to melt). Put the long brownie strip onto a freezerproof serving platter or baking tray, then pile the ice cream on top and quickly neaten the sides and top. Arrange the 8 brownie pieces on top. Return to the freezer until firm then wrap tightly and freeze for at least 6 hours before serving.

When ready to serve, use a sharp knife to cut into 8 portions and offer a jug of Creamy Chocolate Sauce (see page 62) for pouring. The assembled cake can be kept in the freezer for up to a week.

Here, a fudgy brownie made with plenty of chocolate and toasted pecans, and baked slightly thinner than usual, is combined with a good ready-made ice cream – either white chocolate or vanilla. Serve with a jug of your choice of hot sauce for pouring.

brownie ice cream

Brownie mixture:

50 g good plain chocolate

50 g unsalted butter

100 g light brown muscovado sugar

½ teaspoon real vanilla essence

1 large free-range egg, lightly beaten

50 g plain flour

1½ tablespoons cocoa powder

75 g pecan pieces, toasted

To finish:

750 ml good-quality white chocolate or vanilla ice cream

a 20.5 x 20.5 cm brownie tin, greased and base-lined
a freezerproof container

Serves 6 to 8

Preheat the oven to 180°C (350°F) Gas 4. First make the brownie mixture: break up the chocolate and put it into a heatproof bowl with the butter. Set over a pan of steaming water and melt gently, stirring frequently.

Remove the bowl from the pan and use a wooden spoon to stir in the sugar and vanilla. Leave to cool for a couple of minutes then stir in the beaten egg.

Sift the flour and cocoa onto the mixture then mix in. When thoroughly combined stir in the nuts. Transfer the mixture to the prepared tin and spread evenly.

Bake in the preheated oven for about 12 to 15 minutes or until just firm to the touch. Leave to cool then remove from the tin.

To finish: chop up the brownie into pieces roughly the size of your thumb nail. Transfer the ice cream to the fridge to soften (without letting it start to melt) then mix in the brownie pieces. Spoon the mixture into a freezerproof container and freeze until firm.

Serve with a jug of hot sauce. Choose from Butterscotch Fudge Sauce, Chocolate Fudge Sauce (see page 61) or Coffee Sauce (see page 62).

sauces

chocolate fudge sauce

A lovely thick and rich hot sauce that's not too sweet.

175 g good-quality plain chocolate
40 g unsalted butter, diced
2 tablespoons golden syrup
175 ml single cream or milk

Makes 4 to 6 servings

Break up the chocolate and put it in a small, heavy-based pan with the butter, golden syrup and cream (or milk).

Set over low heat and melt gently, stirring constantly. Continue stirring and heating until the mixture is almost at boiling point. Pour into a warmed jug and serve immediately.

The sauce will thicken as it cools but can be gently reheated.

Any leftover sauce can be covered and stored in the fridge for up to 2 days. Reheat gently before using.

butterscotch fudge sauce

A deliciously rich sauce. Good served with blondies.

90 g unsalted butter, diced
200 g dark or light brown muscovado sugar
2 tablespoons golden syrup
90 ml double cream

Makes 6 servings

Put the butter, sugar and golden syrup in a small, heavy-based pan. Melt gently over very low heat, stirring frequently, until the sugar dissolves completely (about 10 minutes).

When smooth and melted, stir in the cream then raise the heat and stir until the sauce is piping hot but not boiling. Pour into a warmed jug and serve immediately.

Any leftover sauce can be covered and stored in the fridge for up to 3 days. Reheat gently before using.

creamy chocolate sauce

A simple yet rich sauce without added sugar.

125 ml double cream
85 g good-quality plain chocolate, chopped
½ teaspoon real vanilla essence

Makes 4 to 6 servings

Pour the cream into a small, heavy-based saucepan and heat gently, stirring frequently. When the cream comes to the boil remove the pan from the heat and let cool for a minute. Stir in the chopped chocolate and vanilla and keep stirring until the sauce is smooth. Pour into a warmed jug and serve immediately.

The sauce will thicken as it cools but can be gently reheated.

Any leftover sauce can be stored, tightly covered, in the fridge for up to 2 days. Reheat very gently, stirring constantly, before using.

white chocolate sauce

Choose top-quality white chocolate flavoured with real vanilla beans (rather than children's bars) for a good rich taste.

200 g good-quality white chocolate

200 ml double cream

80 ml milk

1 vanilla bean

Makes 4 to 6 servings

Break up the chocolate and put it in a heatproof bowl, set over a pan of steaming water.

Allow to melt gently, stirring frequently. Remove the bowl from the pan and leave to cool until needed.

Put the cream and milk into a small, heavy-based pan. Split the vanilla bean lengthways (to expose the tiny seeds inside) and add to the pan. Heat, stirring constantly, until scalding hot but not quite boiling.

Remove from the heat and leave to stand for 5 minutes. Remove the vanilla bean then pour the hot cream and milk onto the melted chocolate in a thin stream, whisking constantly, to make a smooth sauce. Pour into a warmed jug and serve immediately.

Any leftover sauce can be stored, tightly covered, in the fridge for up to 2 days. Reheat very gently, stirring constantly.

coffee sauce

Use good, well-flavoured coffee but not espresso (or dilute espresso until it tastes like filter or cafétiere coffee).

100 g good plain chocolate

60 g unsalted butter, diced

100 ml good coffee

Makes 4 to 6 servings

Break up the chocolate and put it in a heatproof bowl. Add the butter and coffee then set the bowl over a pan of steaming water.

Allow to melt gently, stirring frequently, until very smooth. Remove the bowl from the pan and stir until glossy and slightly thickened. As the sauce cools it will become even thicker. Serve warm.

Any leftover sauce can be stored, tightly covered, in the fridge for up to 2 days. Reheat very gently, stirring constantly.

index